IMAGES OF NATURE

OHIO

JERRY SIEVE

FOREWORD BY SENATOR HOWARD METZENBAUM

WESTCLIFFE PUBLISHERS, INC. ENGLEWOOD, COLORADO

CONTENTS

Foreword	7
Preface	11
Color	14
Form	32
Moment	50
Place	64
Microcosm	80
Light	94
Technical Information	112

International Standard Book Number:
 ISBN 0-929969-33-2
Library of Congress Catalogue Card Number: 89-52040
Copyright, Photographs and Text: Jerry Sieve, 1990.
 All rights reserved.
Editor: John Fielder
Assistant Editor: Margaret Terrell Morse
Production Manager: Mary Jo Lawrence
Typographers: Dianne Borneman and Richard M. Kohen
Printed in Korea by Sung In Printing Company, Ltd.,
 Seoul
Published by Westcliffe Publishers, Inc.
 2650 South Zuni Street
 Englewood, Colorado 80110

No portion of this book, either photographs or text, may be reproduced in any form without the written permission of the publisher.

Bibliography

Banta, R.E. *The Ohio Valley: A Student's Guide to Localized History.* New York: Teachers College Press, Columbia University, 1966. Reprinted with permission; see pp. 20, 60.
Banta, R.E. *Rivers of America: The Ohio.* New York: Henry Holt Company, 1949. Reprinted with permission; see p. 48.
Carpenter, Allan. *Ohio, From Its Glorious Past to the Present.* Chicago: Childrens Press, Inc., 1963. Reprinted with permission including the Christopher Gist quotation on pp. 42-43.
Havighurst, Walter. *Ohio, A History.* New York: W.W. Norton & Company, Inc., 1976. Reprinted with permission including the J.M. Peck quotation on p. 36.
Santmyer, Helen Hooven. *Ohio Town.* New York: Harper & Row, Publishers, Inc., 1984. Reprinted with permission.

First Frontispiece: Early morning at Blue Hen Falls,
 Cuyahoga Valley National Recreation Area,
 Summit County
Second Frontispiece: White oak in spring flush,
 Glen Helen Nature Preserve, Greene County
Title Page: Fallen apples and dried grasses,
 Lucas County
Right: Early snow accented by fallen leaves in
 Mitchell Memorial Forest, Hamilton County

HOWARD METZENBAUM
FOREWORD

Long before our forefathers set foot on the North American continent, geologic and other natural forces combined to create a land diverse in beauty and environment. As our populations and cultures have grown and matured, a relationship has been cultivated with our natural surroundings. In Ohio, the development of communities and the evolution of local cultures have been defined by the natural environment.

For the casual visitor, Ohio often conjures up ageless images of peaceful rural communities reminiscent of Sherwood Anderson's *Winesburg, Ohio*. Communities formed in response to the idyllic and benevolent surroundings. Communities as timeless as the environment that preceded them.

Ohio's geographic features have created a natural environment abundant with diversity. The winding Ohio River in the southern reaches of the state not only defines the southern border of Ohio, but has shaped and formed its distinctive geography over a period spanning thousands of years. Lake Erie, the bustling waterway in the north, has demarcated not only the northern border of Ohio, but has provided a source of livelihood for many generations.

While Lake Erie has been a corridor for commercial and industrial activity, the state's rolling hills and sprawling fields have created an amiable climate for its farmers. For decades, the Ohio farmer has tilled the land and coaxed the earth to produce a bounty worth sharing at his neighbor's table, a bounty defined by man's relationship with his natural surroundings.

At the same time that Ohio's natural environment has fostered a productive and flourishing relationship with its working citizens, the state's recreational resources appear limitless. The opportunities available to outdoor enthusiasts in Ohio, from Kelleys Island to Wayne National Forest, seem limited only by the imagination.

A walk along a secluded riverbank or a bicycle ride through the hills remain two of my favorite activities in Ohio's gentle yet majestic outdoors. Since 1976 I have represented the people of Ohio in the United States Senate. As my travels have taken me to every corner of this great state, I have become increasingly familiar with and appreciative of Ohio's natural splendor.

Yet, as we close the chapter on the 20th century and continue to expand our populations, we need to take stock of the condition of our natural surroundings. The land has lost its resilience in the face of years of exploitation and wanton disregard. It remains one of my greatest fears that the natural environment we have taken for granted may become a mere image of the past.

We have and must continue to sow the seeds of a relationship with our natural surroundings founded more on respect and less on dominance. In our efforts to establish goals to protect our environment we should focus on entering the 21st century with the priority of preserving our natural environments for coming generations to enjoy and respect.

— HOWARD METZENBAUM
U.S. Senator, Ohio

Tumbling cascade at Sharon Woods Gorge State Nature Preserve, Hamilton County
Overleaf: Dame's rocket wildflowers brighten a shady glen, Pickaway County

JERRY SIEVE
PREFACE

Many young people, in their hurry to grow up, look at the world around them but don't really *see* anything. I certainly fell into this category. While growing up in the Western Hills area of Cincinnati, I rarely left the "Hill." Most of my first 20 years was spent within about a six-square-mile area, insulated from much of what was "out there."

It wasn't until the third decade of my life that I began to develop a vision of the world around me. About the same time I started developing an interest in photography. This need to capture images on film—combined with a growing wanderlust—laid the groundwork for my photographic career, which began several years later.

When I returned to Ohio in 1988 to photograph for this book, I wondered what I would find. As a 40-year-old westerner, how would I see the state where I had spent 20 of the first 24 years of my life? I sensed that I would be discovering Ohio for the first time.

It was mid-April when I drove into southern Ohio from Indiana. The deciduous trees had begun leafing out and the dogwood trees were blooming. As I drove across the state I discovered that spring meant something different to me than it had when I was young. It was no longer just a time that marked warmer weather and the end of the school year. Spring had become a time of pale greens, blossoming trees and grasses pushing through the moist earth.

As I returned to Ohio again and again, I discovered that each season has its own attraction for the photographer. Winter's dramatic ice falls and skeletal forms, spring's showy displays of flowers, summer's humid air and lush vegetative growth. But autumn was the season I enjoyed the most. I found the cool air and vibrant colors intoxicating. Photographically, there are not many scenes in nature more stunning than maple trees in full fall splendor.

In all, 20 weeks of work went into the production of images for this book. I made seven different trips, covering each season twice except for summer. It took more than 15,000 miles on Ohio's many roads and trails to visit the more than 75 areas that I photographed, some in each of the four seasons.

Photographing the land of my birth was a challenge after living in the West for 15 years. Lacking the broad vistas, big skies and dry air of the West, Ohio has its own, more subtle, beauty.

Much of Ohio's contemporary landscape is devoted to agricultural production. There is no doubting the ability of the state's agrarian community to produce an abundance of food. I don't think I've ever tasted corn so sweet and delicate. Ohio's farms help feed its cities, the state, the country, the world.

The landform of Ohio is largely the result of the most recent ice age. It was sculpted by the direct action of massive ice flows and by the drainage and debris of retreating glaciers.

A fertile lowland known as the Great Lakes Plains covers a narrow strip of land bordering Lake Erie in the northern part of the state. A few low, sandy ridges and fossil beaches—remnants of post-glacial Lake Erie—break the flatness. The western portion of this lowland contains most of the Maumee River drainage system.

To the southwest lie the gently rolling hills of the Till Plains, the easternmost portion of the great midwestern Corn Belt. This fertile farmland is marked in places by waterfalls that descend dramatic cliffs gouged from the limestone bedrock.

The Appalachian Plateau covers most of the eastern half of Ohio. To the north are rolling hills and valleys. The southern two-thirds of this highland, untouched by the glaciers, is marked by steep hills and valleys. This rugged region is home to the state's largest forests.

Once, it was said, a squirrel could move from one end of Ohio to the other and never touch the ground. Before the coming of the white man, the region that is now Ohio laid claim to what may have been the largest deciduous hardwood forest in the world. The early pioneers discovered that the soil was much thicker and richer than that found in New England. When the word spread, the rush was on. Tree by tree the land was cleared, to the point that today only a few acres remain of this vast virgin forest.

Kelleys Island catches the sun's last rays, Lake Erie

It is estimated that 99 percent of Ohio's natural landscape has been altered by human settlement. As a result of all of this change, more than 200 of the state's plants are considered endangered while another 200 are threatened with destruction.

The pressure on ecosystems continues on many fronts. Strip-mines ravage the hills to the southeast. I have seen clear-cutting of forest in what I consider to be one of the state's most scenic areas, the Hocking Hills. Many of Ohio's wetlands are gone or are under severe pressure from nearby development. This is especially true along the Lake Erie shoreline.

But, fortunately, all is not lost, and Ohioans have plenty still to be proud of. Within a short distance of just about every area of the state there is a preserve where people can see Ohio's natural beauty as it has been and, hopefully, as it always will be.

The Ohio Department of Natural Resources has set aside 90 nature preserves and 11 scenic rivers. The Nature Conservancy and other private groups also have landholdings throughout the state and are working diligently toward the preservation of others. These areas, which vary in size from less than an acre to thousands of acres, are ecologically and geologically significant laboratories of Ohio's natural heritage.

There will always be forces within the state who want to develop every square inch of land for the sake of economic progress. These individuals believe that land has no value unless cutting, extracting or developmental "enhancement" can take place. But I have met many Ohioans who feel differently. They believe there is intrinsic value in land left undisturbed. They do not see the earth as a means to monetary gain. The beauty of trillium in spring or the magnificent eroded shapes of Black Hand sandstone have helped form their personal philosophies about the world around them.

What can you do to help preserve Ohio's natural beauty? Concerned residents can make a difference. Support your local environmental groups by finding out their concerns for the threatened areas of the state. Write to your state and federal representatives with your opinions about questionable actions and developments. Some activities near parks or natural areas can threaten their ecological integrity. Let the powers that be know what you think. It works! I know Ohioans who have gotten action from their words.

I would like to see the establishment and preservation of areas that retain some of their original wildness. These lands would give Ohioans a chance to experience the state as it existed more than 300 years ago, providing a basis for reflection on Ohio's past and future.

I have learned much about Ohio from its gracious people, but even more from the land itself. I have learned that the state's natural areas are worth protecting. From fields of wildflowers and life-sustaining wetlands to secluded hollows and water-carved gorges, each has value in its natural state. I leave you with my images of Ohio. Give them a good long look. It is my hope that through them Ohio's natural values will become apparent, making their own case for preservation.

—JERRY SIEVE

To my wife, Kevina, my companion in life.

Frosty morning, Ross County

COLOR

The simple use of color can add to an image's presence in several ways. Color can tell the viewer what time of year it is and to a certain extent what time of day it is. As the angle of the sun changes by the month and by the hour, the colors in a landscape vary from warm to cool and back again. As the seasons progress, the bright yellow-greens of spring give way to summer's deep greens and autumn's browns, yellows and oranges.

In some cases, color serves as more than just an accent that lends meaning to an image. Nature's colors can be so powerful that they become their own justification. Azure skies, wildly colored flowers, painted stone cliffs—all create images in their own right.

While in the field, the photographer searches for color that will produce a strong emotional response in the viewer. The interplay of cool color against warm is one of the nature photographer's stronger compositional tools.

The human eye perceives color in a different way than film does, by mentally filtering out any shift in color caused by the time of day or reflected hues. Color film faithfully records all of these variations. What is considered "good" color depends on the photographer's intent. "Natural" color might be how the scene is perceived by the eye. However, "accurate" color can be aesthetically pleasing regardless of how normal or "natural" the colors appear. These colors can be achieved by becoming aware of how various lighting and weather conditions affect the natural landscape.

Left: Evening settles over Stewart Lake, Scioto Trail State Park, Ross County
Above: Dame's rockets and field mustard, Marion County

"I passed the spring, summer and autumn of life among the trees. The winter of my days had come, and found me where I loved to be, —in the quiet way—ay, and in the honesty of the woods. . . ." —James Fenimore Cooper

Trees begin their seasonal color swing, Conkles Hollow State Nature Preserve, Hocking County

Barn in early spring, Richland County

"Other patches of woodland were more varied than the streamside trees: nearby stands were brilliantly multicolored in the fall, and in the spring more delicately so; the line along the horizon was amethystine in October and April, indigo in the light of midsummer." — Helen Hooven Santmyer

Spring comes to the rolling hills of Shawnee State Forest, Scioto County

Blooming asters and goldenrod dot a field in Maumee Bay State Park, Ottawa County

"Somewhere [the Mound Builders] had learned to farm... and they raised and preserved corn, kidney beans, squash, pumpkins... every one of which originated in the Americas, was unknown to Europeans before Columbus, and is... very satisfactory eating." — R.E. Banta

Piled pumpkins demonstrate nature's bounty, Henry County

Tulip trees and red maples in spring, Conkles Hollow State Nature Preserve, Hocking County

"There was not always time to go on to the second, farther woods, but if there were, you found it even more beautiful than the first, and if you saw it in the one brief perfect hour of spring, you hung transfixed on the top rail of the fence. In that hour the redbuds were past their prime, paler than in their first brightest flowering." — Helen Hooven Santmyer

Redbud blossoms herald the arrival of spring, Shawnee State Park, Scioto County

Purple coneflowers punctuate the lush greens of Smith Cemetery Prairie, Madison County
Overleaf: Autumn forest frames Tinkers Creek Gorge National Natural Landmark,
Cleveland Metro Parks, Cuyahoga County

Fire pinks blossom on forest floor, Conkles Hollow State Nature Preserve, Hocking County

Overlooking Brandywine Falls, Cuyahoga Valley National Recreation Area

Early snow on coral berry bush, Hamilton County

Field of blooming lupine, the Nature Conservancy's Kitty Todd Preserve, Lucas County

Maple tree celebrates autumn in Mitchell Memorial Forest, Hamilton County

Descent of Yellow Spring in Glen Helen Nature Preserve, Greene County

FORM

Form is an organizational tool in the design of a photograph. It is the arrangement of positive and negative space on film that leads the viewer's eyes across an image. Often we are drawn to the edges of these shapes, as in silhouettes. Textural qualities, as well, can contribute to the form of a photographic subject.

If form means shape, it also implies a third dimension. By noticing the effects of perspective—the way shadows fall, the overlapping of near and far shapes—the photographer can help control the way an image presents itself. Careful use of natural light is another excellent tool in the definition of form.

Form helps to set the relationship among the various elements in an image. Humans appreciate rhythms—day and night, the seasons, the human heartbeat—because of their prevalence in nature. Possibly because of this, the brain looks for ways to simplify visual messages, which is why people respond to balance and organization in a photographic image. From afar, nature's forms are myriad and confusing. Upon closer inspection, the photographer can find ways to convey his message through careful pictorial arrangement.

Left: Oak tree silhouetted by setting winter sun, Mount Echo Park, Hamilton County   Above: Wagon wheels at Hale Farm and Village blacksmith's shop, Summit County

"For the... rail fence, zigzagging around a field or garden, the best woods were ash, oak, walnut, chestnut, and poplar. The rail-splitter used wedges, of iron and wood, driven into the grain of an eight-foot log. The log was halved, quartered, often double-quartered, and finally the heartwood was split off for an extra rail." — Walter Havighurst

Early spring at Rockbridge State Nature Preserve, Hocking County

Split-rail fence and fallen leaves, Mitchell Memorial Forest, Hamilton County

"Such an extent of forest has never before been cleared, such a vast field of prairies was never before subdued and cultivated by the hand of man in the same short period of time. Cities and towns and villages and counties and states never before rushed into existence and made such giant strides." —J.M. Peck

Cultivated rows of a bean field, Madison County

Barren tree branches in Hatch–Otis State Nature Preserve, Lake County

"And under your feet are thick unstable tussocks of grass, liquid mud that gurgles as you move.... Cattails in the spring were last year's crop, winter-killed and brittle...."
— Helen Hooven Santmyer

New growth emerges beneath dried grasses at the Nature Conservancy's Kitty Todd Preserve, Lucas County

Reeds in swamp ice, Cuyahoga Valley National Recreation Area, Summit County
Overleaf: Columbine wildflowers bloom in Charleston Falls Preserve, Miami County

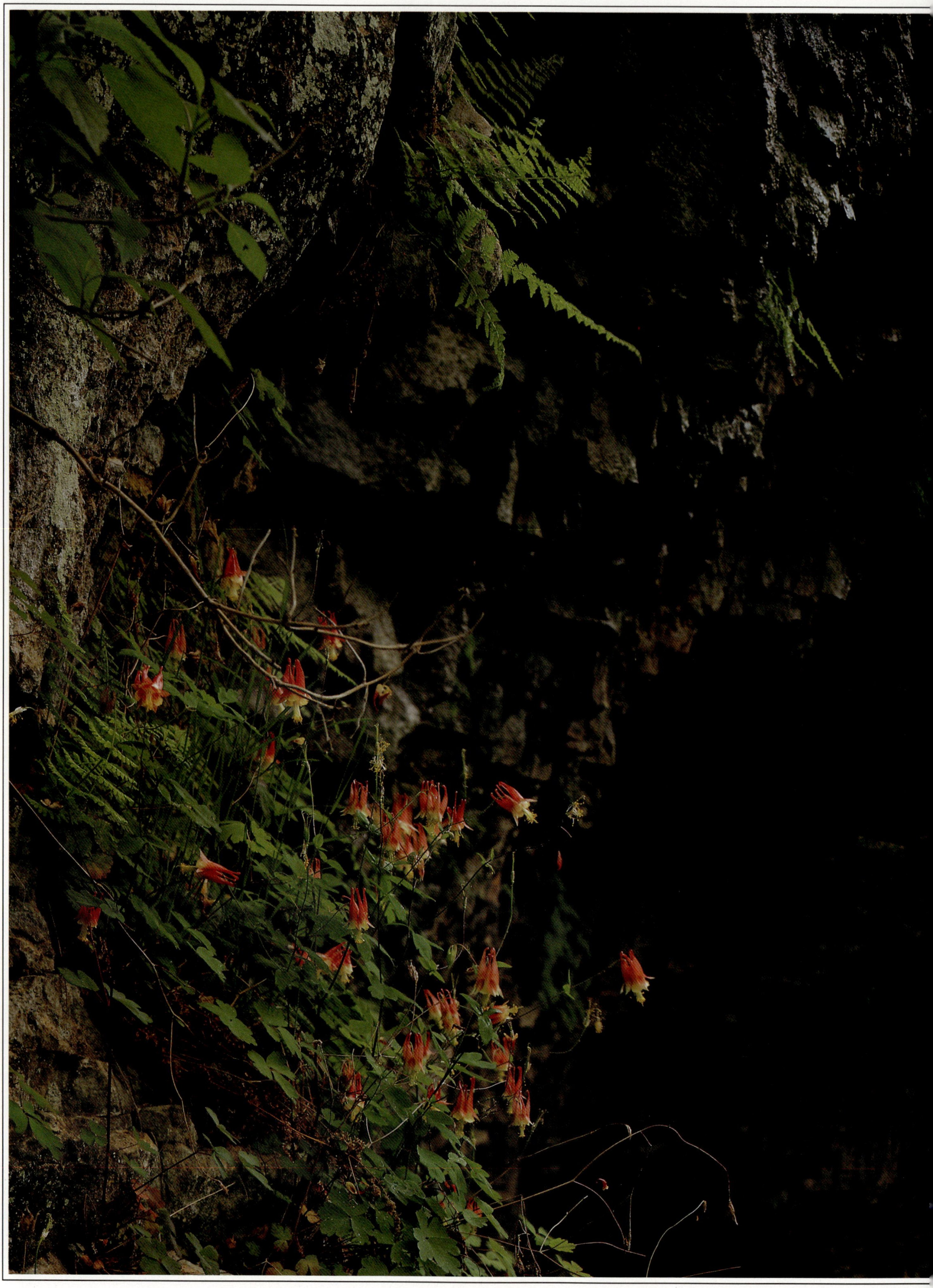

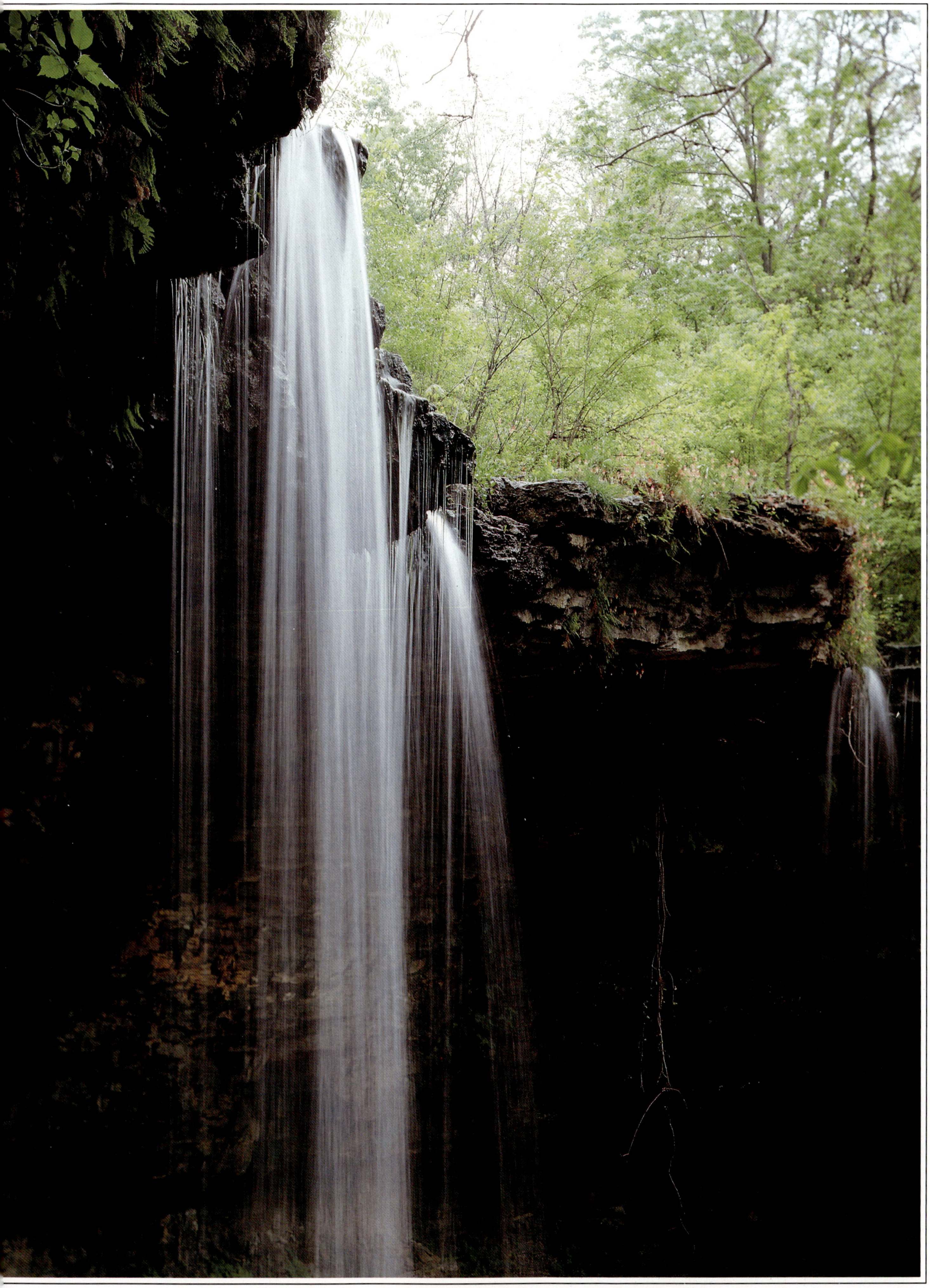

"The Ohio Country is fine, rich, level land, well-timbered with large walnut, ash, sugar trees, cherry trees, etc. It is well watered with a great number of little streams or rivulets, and full of beautiful natural meadows . . .

Rapids along the Greenville State Scenic River, Darke County

"... covered with wild rye, blue grass and clover, and abounds with turkeys, deer, elk and most sorts of game.... In short, it wants nothing but cultivation to make it a most delightful country." — Christopher Gist

Rolled hay bales dot field, Columbiana County

"... the dogwood boughs lay like thin level clouds, white as snow, across the tender green of young-leaved trees, and all the ground below . . . was carpeted with wild phlox . . . everywhere airy and delicate, with the faintest breath of fragrance." — Helen Hooven Santmyer

Dogwood blossoms signal the arrival of spring, Shawnee State Forest, Scioto County

Cedar Falls at Hocking Hills State Park, Hocking County

"Covered bridges belong to the day of the stables long since vanished from our back yards. . . . Because of its associations, a covered bridge seems to be haunted by echoes of the slow clomp-clomp of horses' hooves on its splintery floor, the squeak of wagon wheels, and the light rattle of a buggy." — Helen Hooven Santmyer

Covered bridge spans the Mohican River in Mohican State Park, Ashland County

"In the autumn, fields were faintly powdered with the green of sprouting wheat.... Pastures were russet and stubble fields a rosy brown, and on every hand stood the wigwams of the corn, diminishing in size toward the horizon...."
— Helen Hooven Santmyer

Harvested corn shocks in the Hocking Hills, Hocking County

"Primitive man followed fairly close after the receding glaciers in this region.... Finding what shelter his necessarily rugged physique required under rock shelves projecting from water-worn cliffs he existed in a [benighted] state...."
— R.E. Banta

Ice-covered Black Hand sandstone near Old Man's Cave, Hocking Hills State Park, Hocking County

Trillium wildflowers blanket forest floor, Fowler Woods State Preserve, Richland County

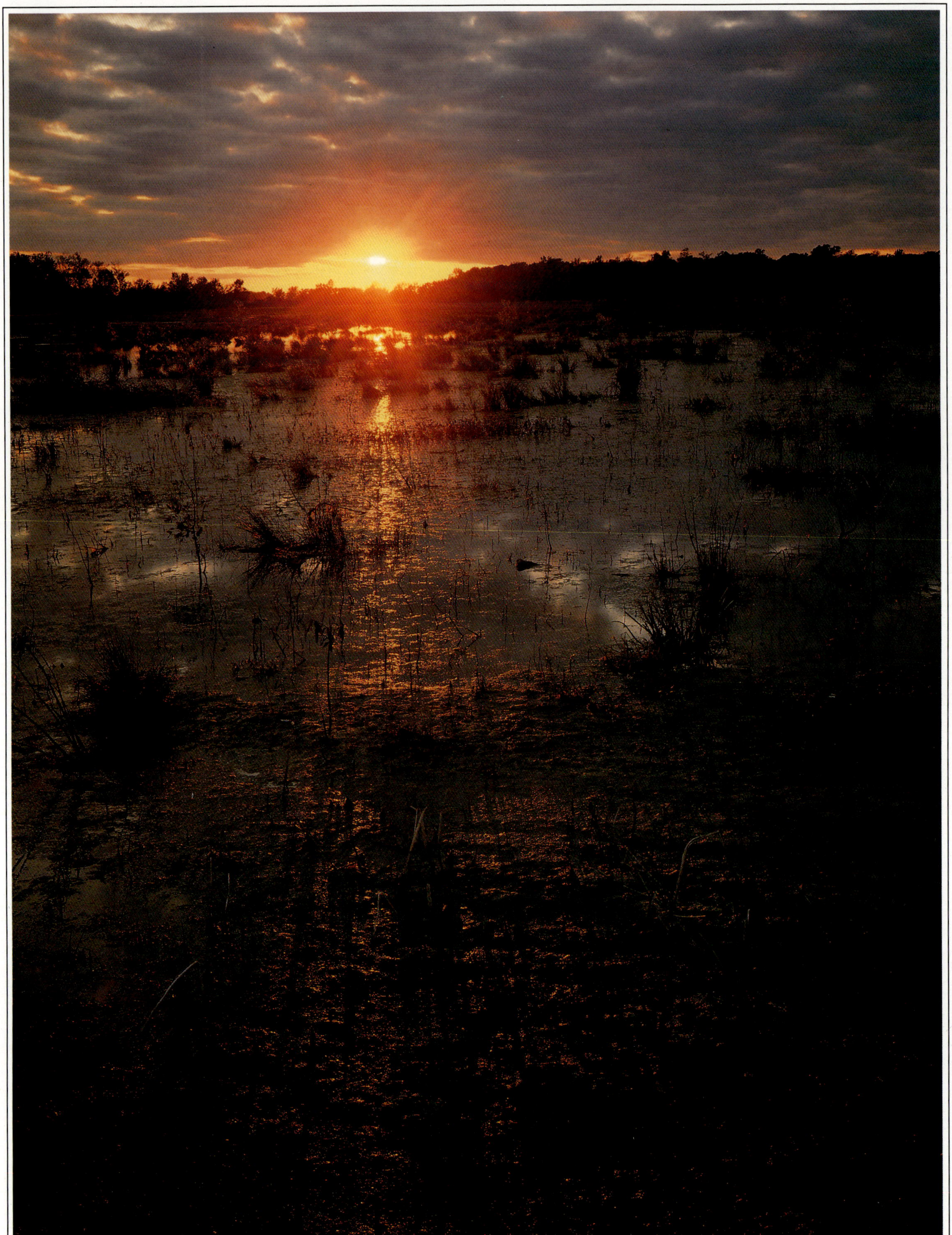

MOMENT

Moments are slices of time in the course of natural history. The photographer's challenge is to be aware of potential moments and to be prepared to respond to the conditions expressed by them. Often these scenes are fleeting, so vigilance is crucial. At times, split-second decisions must be made to take advantage of the interplay of light with the landscape. In these cases, it is helpful to make a mental preconception of the image.

The photographer strives to record with clarity special moments in time and space that many people are not fortunate enough to experience. Such moments may occur in some places every day or for an entire season, while in other locations they may be the result of dramatic weather conditions. During my visual exploration of Ohio, I was honored to experience numerous memorable phenomena—the Ohio sun knifing through autumn-shaded trees, the special atmospheric effects in the Cuyahoga Valley, the colorful seconds just before sunset at Ottawa National Wildlife Refuge.

Left: Autumn sunset at Ottawa National Wildlife Refuge, Ottawa County
Above: Evening light on a sassafras grove, Oak Openings Park, near Toledo

"When white men entered Ohio, it was a forest realm containing 6,700 acres of lakes. Now its lakes cover 100,000 acres. Ohio has 3,300 named streams.... With its gift of rarely failing rainfall Ohio is a well watered land." — Walter Havighurst

Evening at Sylvan Lake, Cuyahoga Valley National Recreation Area, Summit County

Sunset over Greenville Falls, Greenville State Scenic River, Darke County

"The sun would be low in the west, the spring wind fresh and cold in your face, the sky an ineffable blue, the high white clouds piling up, sailing away." — Helen Hooven Santmyer

---

Golden fields under drifting cirrus clouds near Logan, Hocking County

Maple and early snow along Muddy Creek, Hamilton County
Overleaf: Mists rise with the sun over the Scioto River, near Chillicothe, Ross County

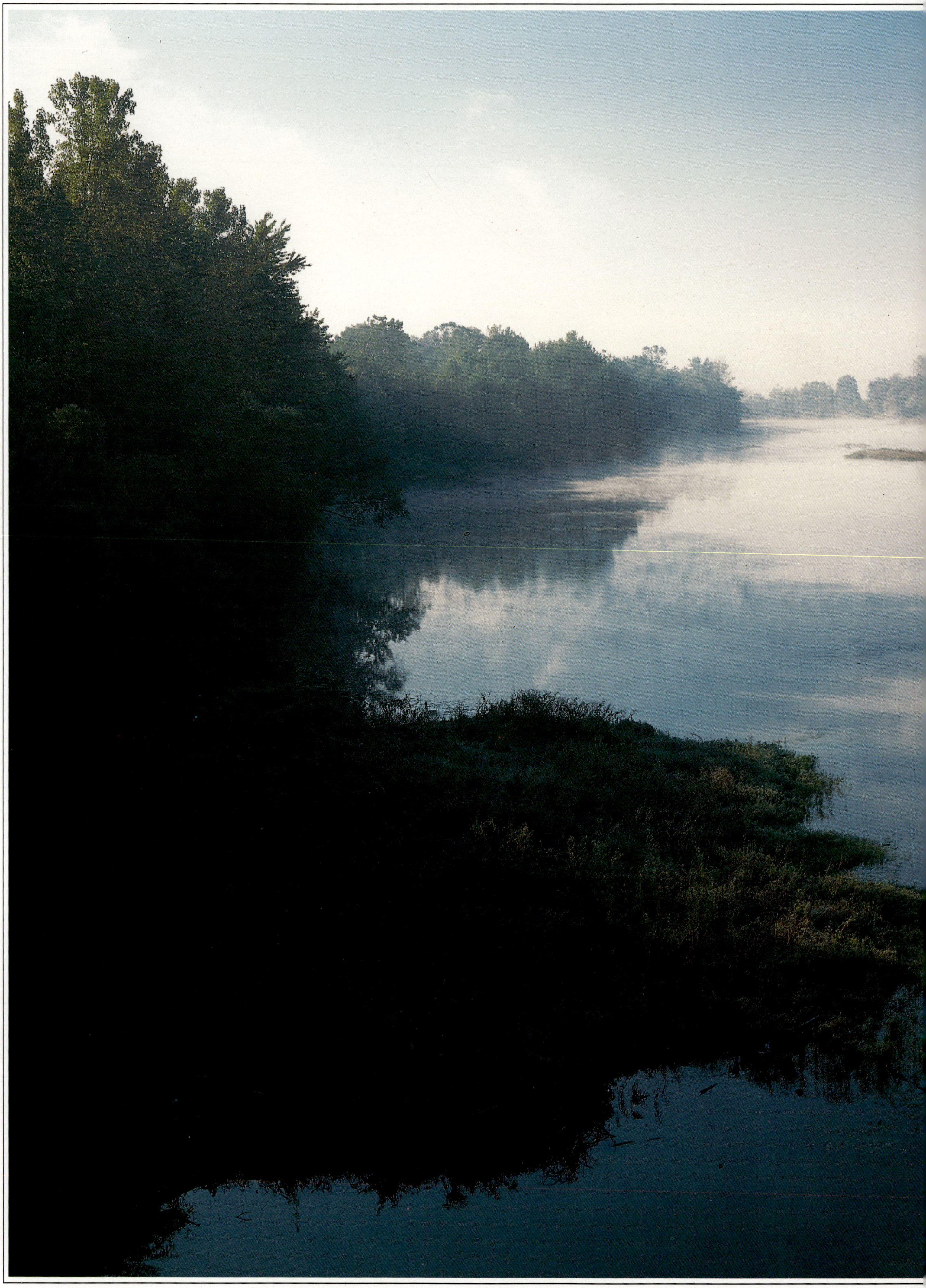

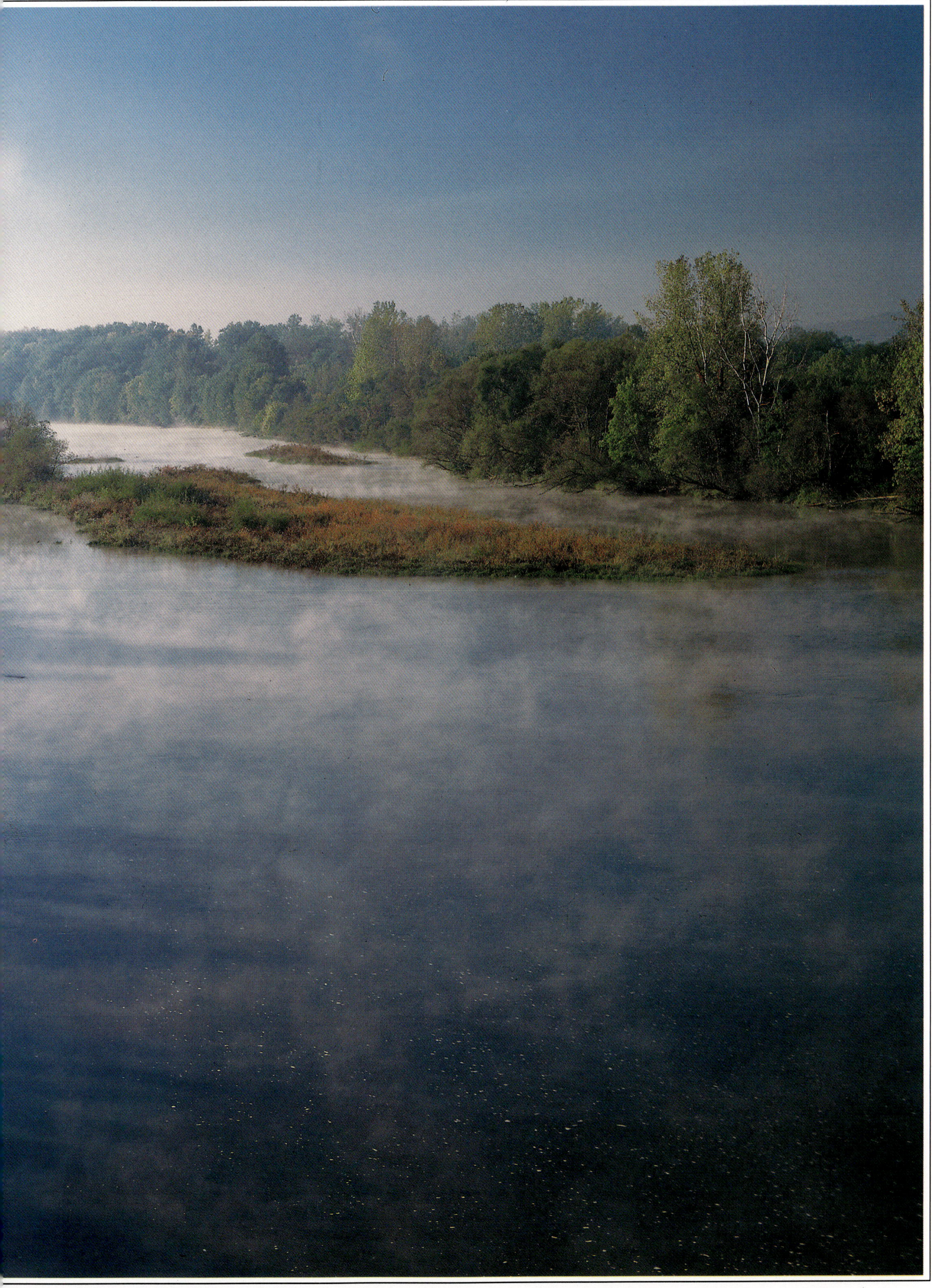

"Hockings State Park is one of Ohio's 80 interesting recreational state parks. At Hockings the visitor sees a rock canyon wilderness as awesome as many in the West, especially surprising in an area so close to so many cities and large towns."
— Allan Carpenter

Ninety-foot descent of waterfall at Ash Cave, Hocking Hills State Park, Hocking County

Ice falls near Old Man's Cave, Hocking Hills State Park, Hocking County

"From time to time through thousands of years great sheets of ice—glaciers—spread down from the Arctic as far south as the Ohio Valley.... There was still... water around from that melting ice... with resulting fogs, rain, snow, and floods a good deal of the time...." — R.E. Banta

Ice-covered stone at Nelson Kennedy Ledges State Park, Portage County

Foggy morning along the Ohio River near Belpre, Washington County

"[*McGuffey's Reader*] saw the brightness of an Ohio morning. Home from school came a first-grader with a poem on the sunrise: 'The lark is up to greet the sun, / The bee is on the wing; / The ant its labors has begun, / The woods with music ring.' " — Walter Havighurst

Dawn over Lake Erie, from Kelleys Island, Erie County

Spring sunset, Richland County

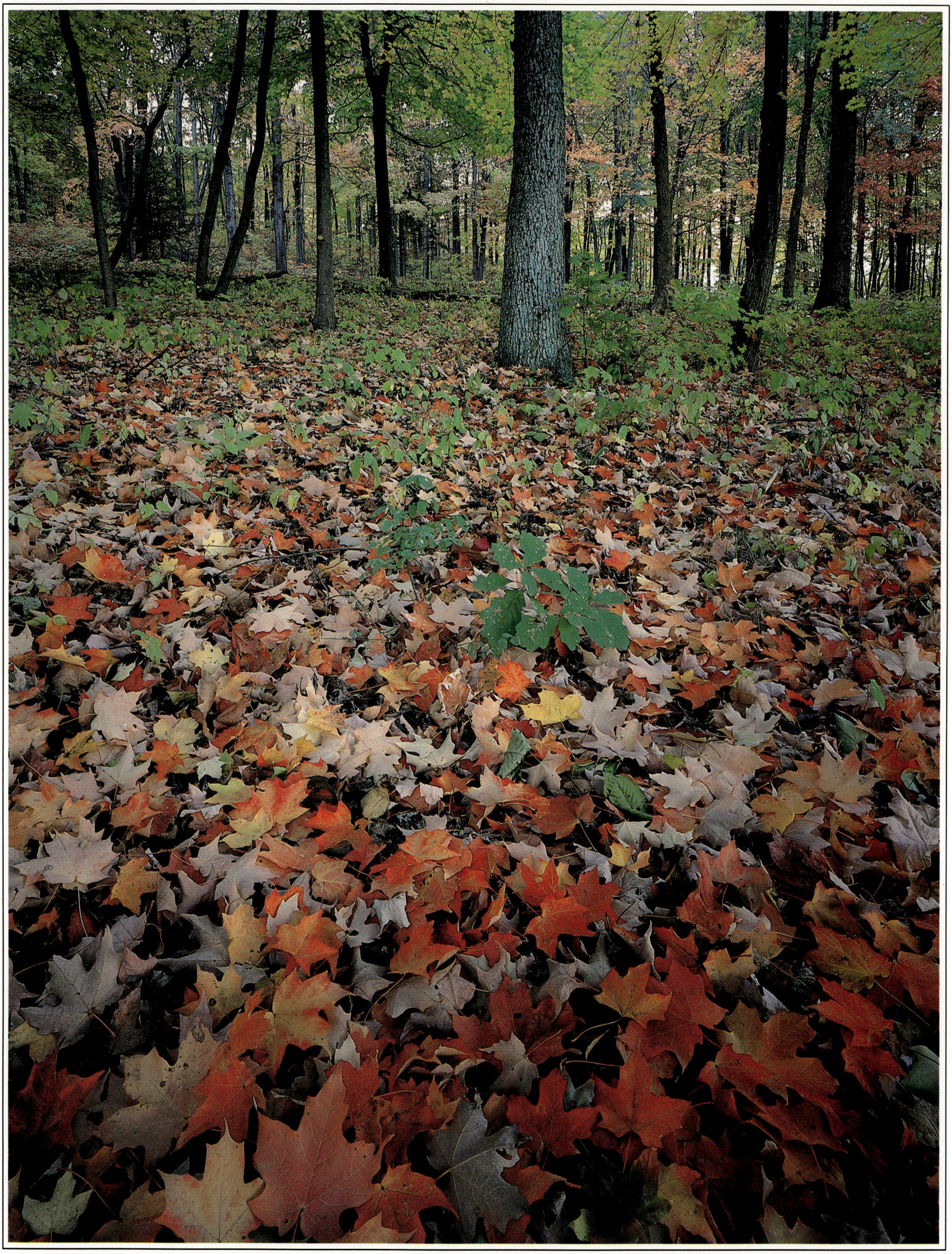

PLACE

It should be easy to photograph a landscape when it's all there—beauty, flowers, leaves, colors, wonderful shapes and textures. Right? Not necessarily. To give an image a sense of place, many variables must be considered. How will the light strike those sandstone cliffs? Is this the correct time of day or year? What about camera angle and height? What is the essence of the subject? What shapes, colors, textures will help define its character?

Images that persuade the viewer to feel a part of the scene help convey a sense of place. A dramatic foreground can give the impression that the viewer can reach out and touch what's in the image. As our environment is assaulted day after day and many photographic subjects are in danger of becoming damaged or completely destroyed, place becomes a critical factor in the purpose of the nature photographer.

Left: Tree seedlings emerge from a blanket of maple leaves, Scioto Trail State Park, Ross County
Above: State Road Bridge spans Conneaut Creek, Ashtabula County

Bluebell wildflowers and skunk cabbage decorate forest floor,
Clearfork Gorge National Natural Landmark, Ashland County

Falls along Birch Creek, Glen Helen Nature Preserve, Greene County

"As [William Henry Harrison] caught the Indian words for hills, woods, plains, waters... his mind filled with pictures of the Ohio country: the meeting of the rivers at Fort Pitt, the dense green of the Big Hocking forest, the great trees... the flint ridges... trails fanning off toward the Ohio River and the great northern lake." — Walter Havighurst

Winter evening on the shores of Lake Erie, Headlands Dunes State Nature Preserve, Lake County

Blossoming phlox in Sharon Woods Gorge State Nature Preserve, Hamilton County

"When we were in a hurry to reach the woods we went . . . to the trees that blurred the horizon, crossing the long sloping meadow and the tilled fields in the early spring when the wheat was just tall enough for its blades to tangle round our ankles . . ." — Helen Hooven Santmyer

Ripening field of grain, Mercer County

Shades of autumn at Gaston's Mill, Beaver Creek State Park, Columbiana County
Overleaf: Leaf-strewn trail in Mitchell Memorial Forest, Hamilton County

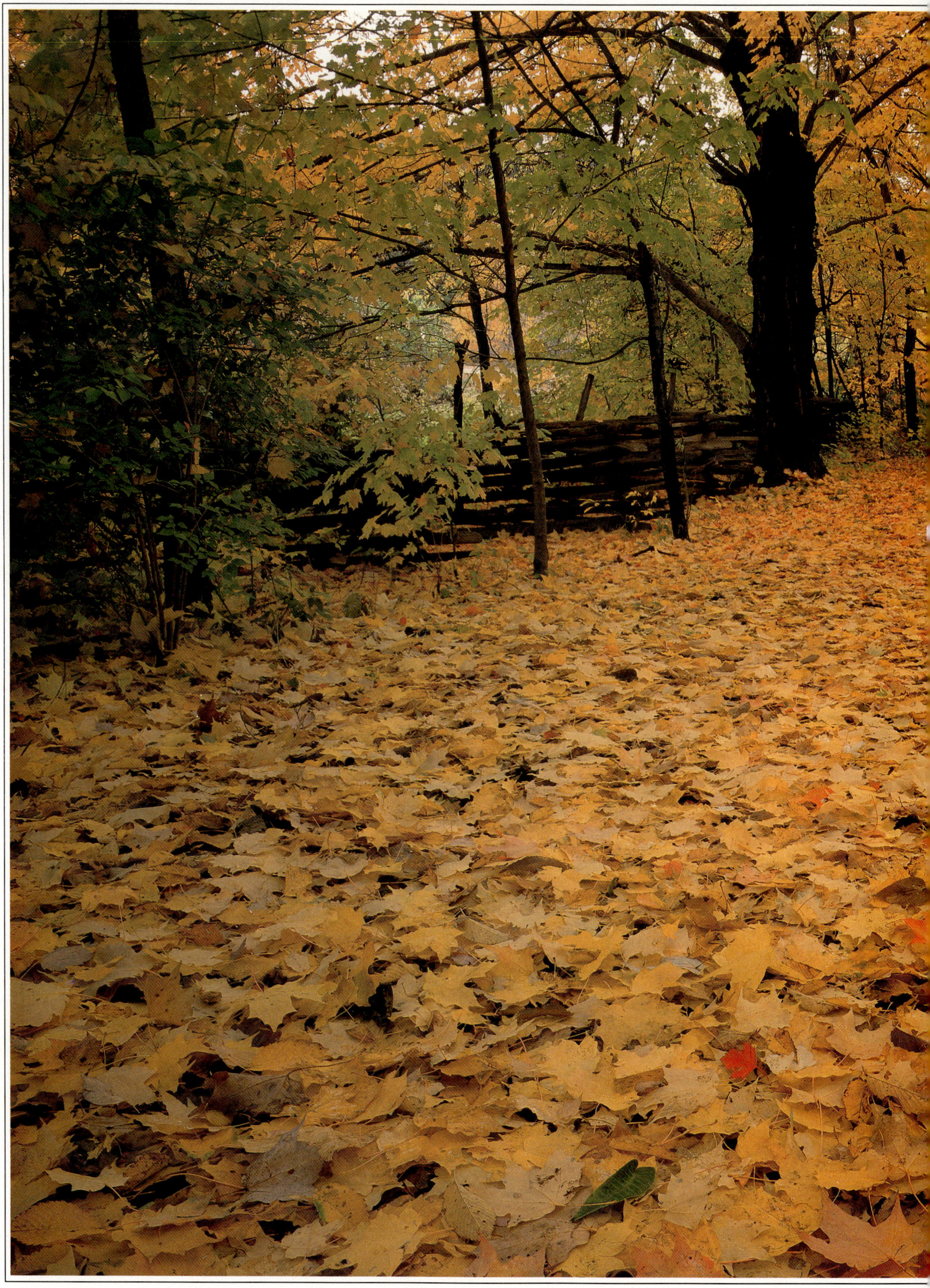

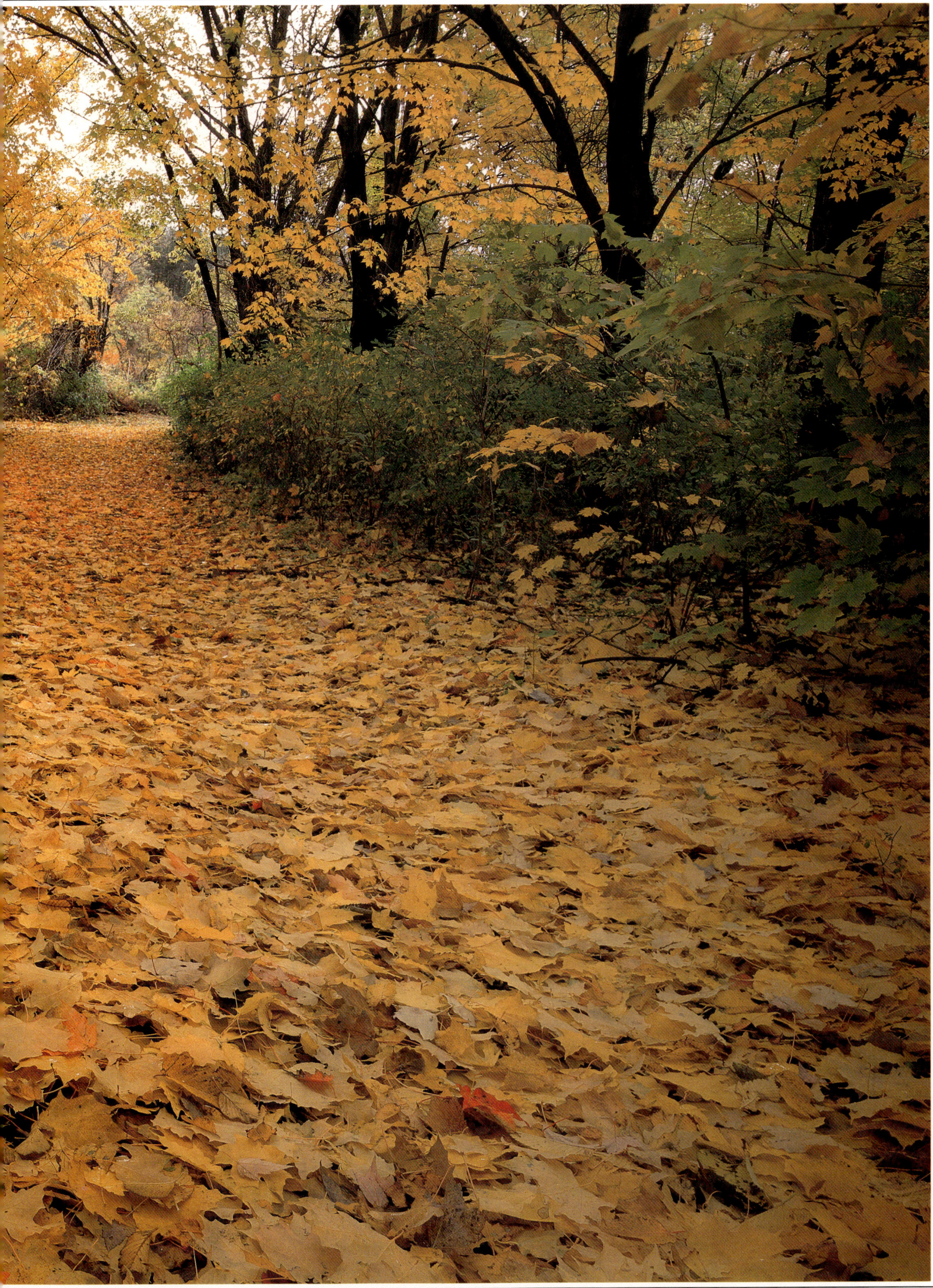

"With winter came the snow, falling white and silent on cabins and cornfields, softening the trails and traces, blanketing the trampled salt licks. . . . It seemed a place removed from history." — Walter Havighurst

---

Oak and hickories on a winter day at Cuyahoga Valley National Recreation Area, Summit County

Rattlesnake master, blazing star and prairie dock brighten Chaparral Prairie, Adams County

Top: Seasonal progression begins with shadows on a winter evening at Conkles Hollow
Bottom: Flowering maple highlights a spring evening, Conkles Hollow State Nature Preserve, Hocking County

Top: Seasonal progression continues with summer trees in full leaf at Conkles Hollow
Bottom: Black Hand sandstone contrasts with brilliant fall colors, Conkles Hollow State Nature Preserve, Hocking County

Remnants of summer confront autumn's approach, Miami–Whitewater Forest, Hamilton County

Last days of summer at Ottawa National Wildlife Refuge, Lucas County

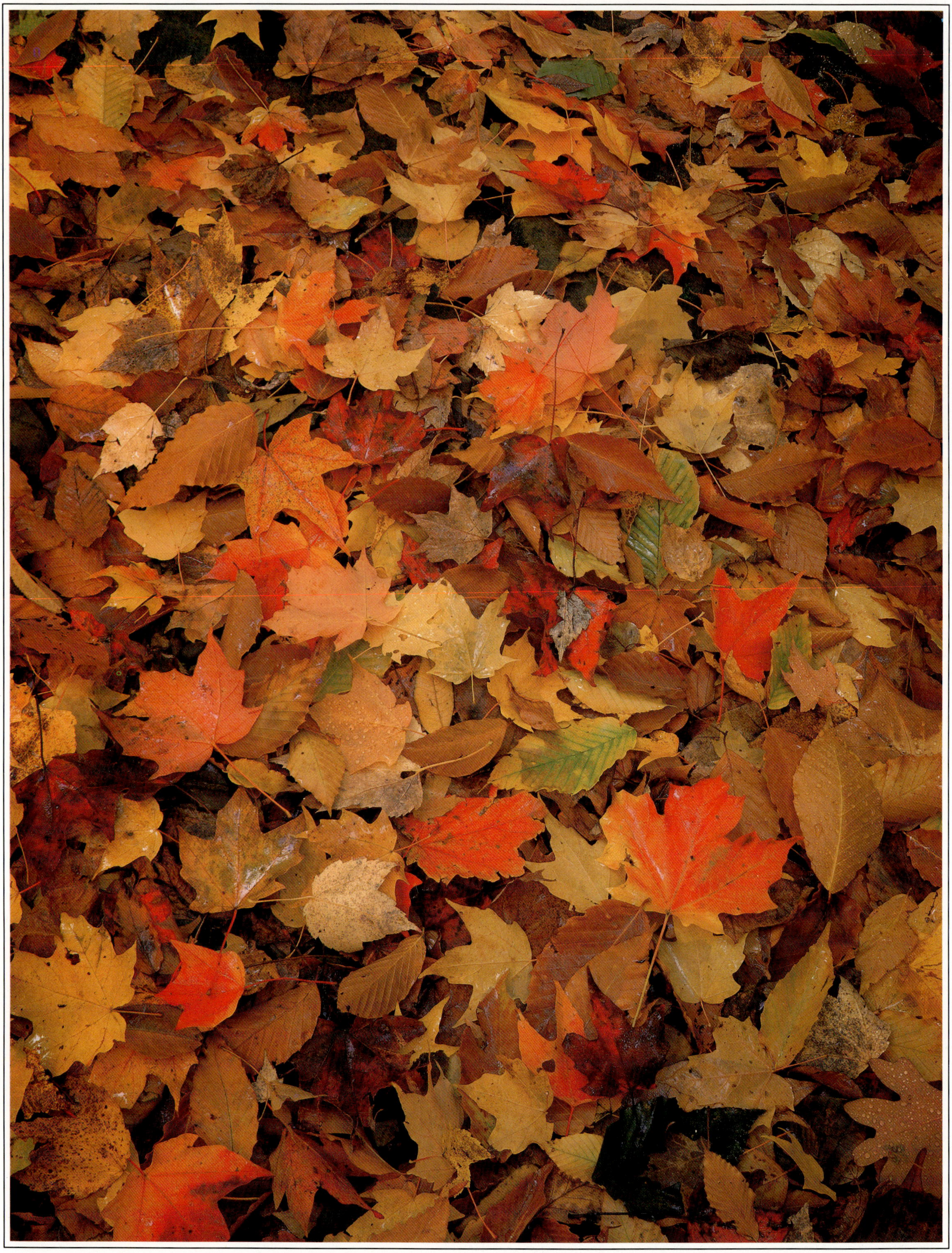

MICROCOSM

Nature's beauty is not just found in the big, the bold and the dramatic. There are myriad worlds waiting to be explored right at our feet. These landscapes in miniature have their own stories to tell.

Microcosms are images that are measured in feet or inches and rarely contain a horizon. Many times they are best photographed in soft light to eliminate the harshness of direct sun, to subtly define shape and to bring out richness of color. Although microcosms may not be as dramatic as big landscapes, they are exciting in their own right. Compositions can be complex—made up of numerous elements—or may include just a single subject or parts of it.

So look down at your feet while exploring the natural world. Be as a child and experience our earth from knee level. See the harmonious yet intricate relationships beneath you, and your vision of nature will expand.

Left: Fallen leaves near Blue Hen Falls, Cuyahoga Valley National Recreation Area, Summit County
Above: Sumac and goldenrod at summer's end, Louis W. Campbell State Nature Preserve, Lucas County

Aged sycamore struggles to produce leaves for another spring, Charleston Falls Preserve, Miami County

Evidence in sandstone of an earlier civilization, Leo Petroglyph State Memorial, Jackson County

Limestone ledges beside Muddy Creek, Hamilton County

Columbine wildflowers at Charleston Falls Preserve, Miami County

"[The soldiers] had marched through wilderness, seeing farms of the future. They talked about sloughs, bogs, bottoms, about clay, loam, and marl. They could judge soil even in dense woods: white oak, walnut, hickory, beech, and sugar maple signify good ground; but never blaze your corners on locust. . . ." — Walter Havighurst

Early morning light on stone barn, Jefferson County

Trillium wildflowers and fallen tree, Clearfork Gorge National Natural Landmark, Ashland County
Overleaf: Prairie coneflowers on Bigelow Cemetery Prairie, Madison County

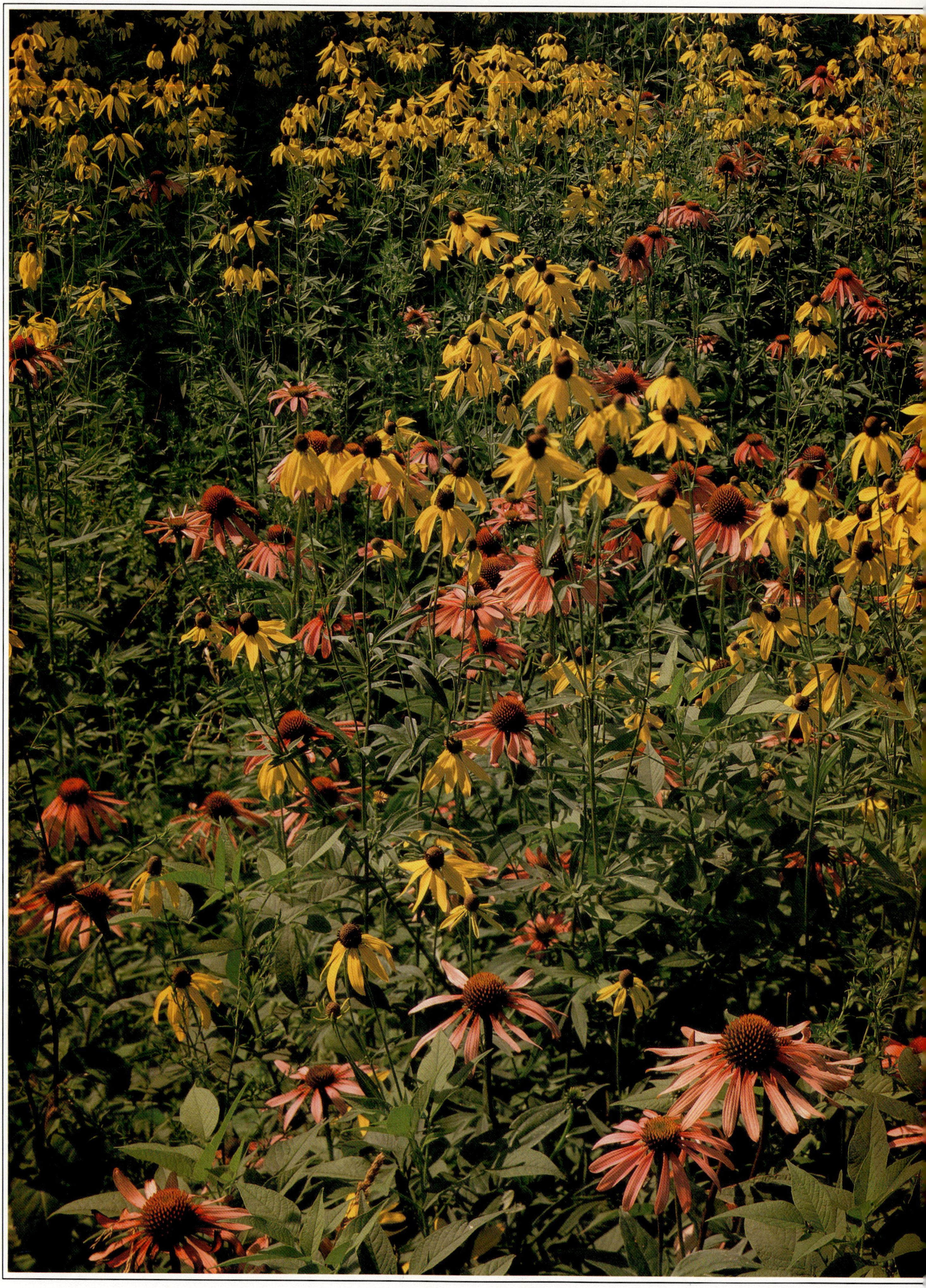

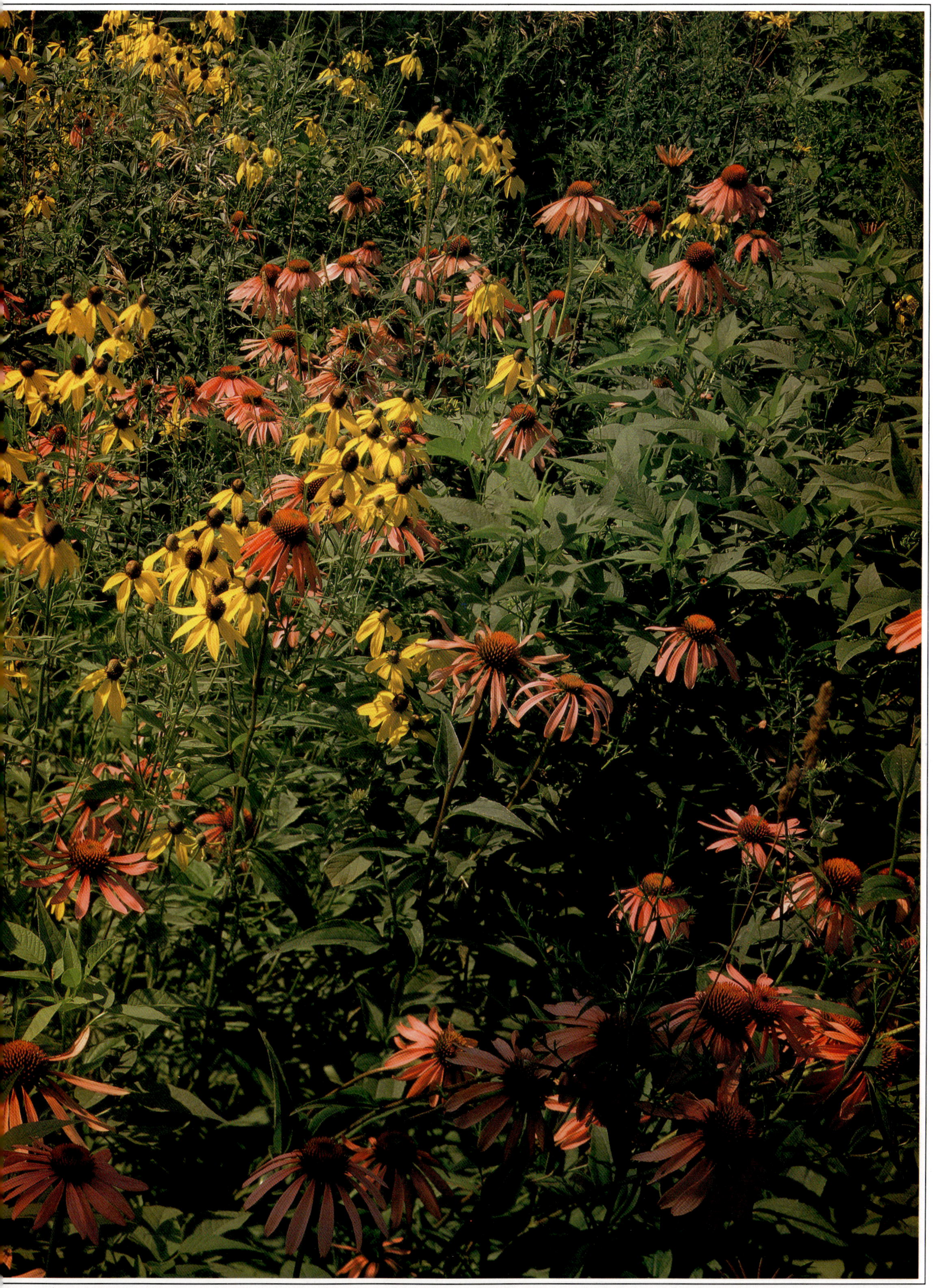

"In the creek itself, darting over the pebbly shallows, hiding at the edge of the bank where the long grass hung down, were minnows and tadpoles. . . . If you wanted minnows or tadpoles, you came to the creek safely by way of the railroad embankment, or, if you were in search of wild flowers, by skirting the edge of the swamp until you reached the bank of the stream east of the low ground."

— Helen Hooven Santmyer

Fall crocus bloom at the Cincinnati Nature Center, Milford, Clermont County

Miniature cascade in Devil's Bathtub at Hocking Hills State Park, Hocking County

Sandstone etchings by pioneers and other visitors at Rock House, Hocking Hills State Park, Hocking County

Fallen leaves and moss-covered rocks at the Ledges Area, Cuyahoga Valley National Recreation Area, Summit County

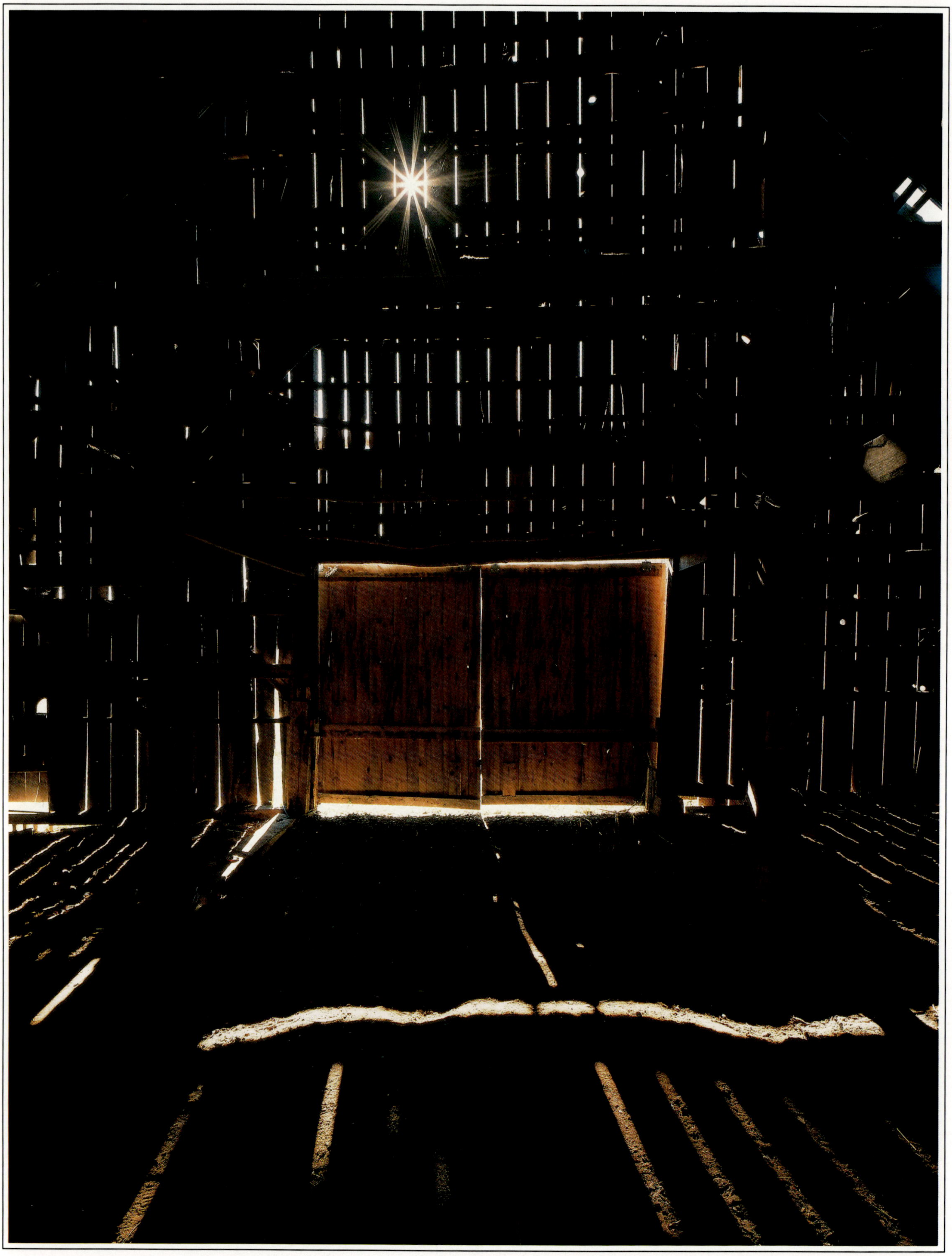

LIGHT

The photographer's control over an image is limited by his most essential tool—light. Unlike the painter who, with the stroke of a brush, can alter the character of light on the canvas, the photographer must take what he finds or wait until the quality of light changes to his satisfaction.

Depending on conditions, the sun can produce many types of light. Hazy sunlight gives a diffused, almost romantic quality to an image. By carefully choosing his position in relation to the light source, the photographer can obtain an ethereal feeling. Reflected and overcast light subtly define shapes and enable the photographer to bring out rich color in an image. Changes in the quality of light give the nature photographer the ability to control the tonal and color characteristics of an image. Light is used to make an image warm or cool, with tones that can be delicate or strong.

Knowledge of light is learned through countless experiences with its effects. By watching through the years, the photographer learns to *see* light. By studying the character of the landscape and being ever-vigilant for the unusual effects of light and atmosphere, the photographer strives to capture his vision on film.

Left: Barn interior, Highland County   Above: Leaning pine trees at cliff side, Conkles Hollow State Nature Preserve, Hocking County

"On golden autumnal Saturdays we passed . . . on the way to gather nuts; with burlap sacks slung over our shoulders we followed the creek to the spot where the hills came close together and were thickly wooded, and among the trees were walnuts and shagbark hickories." — Helen Hooven Santmyer

Autumn-tinged maple in Mitchell Memorial Forest, Hamilton County

Sun burns off morning mist in the Miami–Whitewater Forest, Hamilton County

Blue-eyed Marys carpet hillside, Richardson Forest Preserve, Hamilton County

Frosty autumn morning at Stewart Lake, Scioto Trail State Park, Ross County

"Yet we walked that way often, spring and fall, because once past the outskirts of town, we came to land that was pleasant to the eye: land that had been tended and cared for and loved long enough to have lost its roughness and the look that so much half-tamed American farming country has of waiting only until everyone's back is turned to go back to wilderness." — Helen Hooven Santmyer

Morning frost lingers in shadows, Ross County

Creek above Bridal Veil Falls, Cleveland Metro Parks, Cuyahoga County

Summer sun sets over farmlands, Butler County

Bedrock grooves carved by retreating glaciers, Kelleys Island, Erie County
Overleaf: Mayapple plants spring from decay of forest floor, Hamilton County

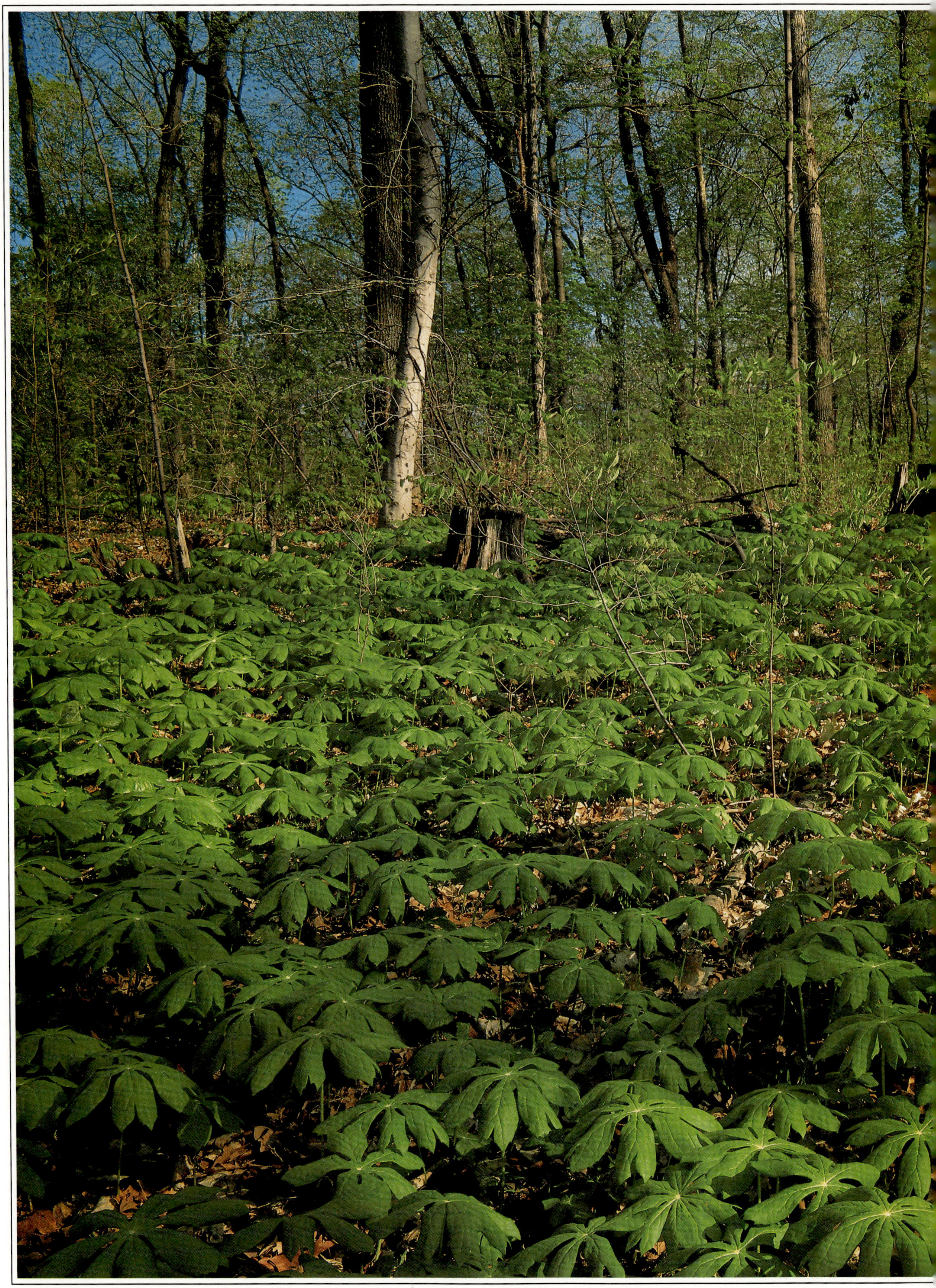

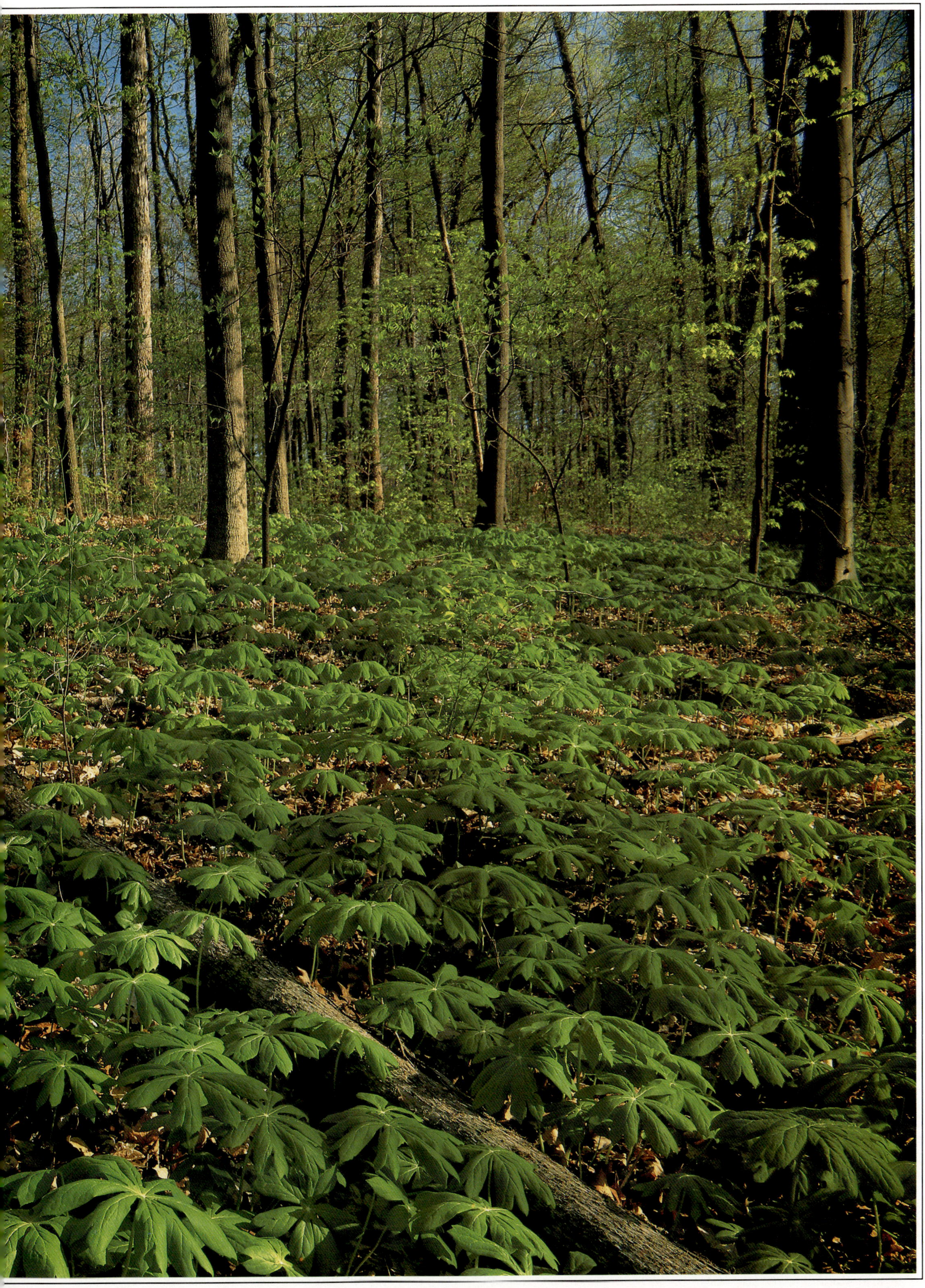

Reflections of early autumn, Tar Hollow State Park, Hocking County

Spring evening at Clifton Gorge State Nature Preserve, Greene County

"Two centuries after the first Ohio axmen began to attack the great forest, Ohio citizens are reclaiming and preserving their natural resources. . . . Ohio, once a destroyer of resources, now asserts some leadership in reforestation, soil-building, restocking of wildlife—a land use that is responsible to the future." — Walter Havighurst

Last light of day, Brown County

Spring blossoms and leaves in Conkles Hollow State Nature Preserve, Hocking County

Greenville State Scenic River tumbles over Greenville Falls, Darke County

Autumn palette at Conkles Hollow State Nature Preserve, Hocking County

Technical Information

All the images in this book were made with a Nagaoka 4x5 field camera, with lenses of 75mm, 135mm, 210mm, 250mm and 540mm focal lengths. Lens apertures ranged from f/22 to f/64, with exposures varying in length from 1/15 second to 60 seconds. Films used were Fujichrome 50 and 100, along with Ektachrome 64 and 100 Plus. Light was measured with a Minolta Spotmeter F. To correct for the blue color cast in open shade, 81 series filters were used with the Ektachrome. No other filtration was used, except for occasional polarization to remove surface reflections. In all cases the scenes were rendered as close as technically possible to how they appeared in nature.

Acknowledgements

I would like to thank Guy Denny and Richard Moseley, from the Ohio Department of Natural Resources, for their guidance and permits while I was photographing the state's natural areas and preserves. I am also grateful to naturalist Ric Queen of Hocking Hills State Park for personally helping me discover some of Ohio's beauty. Finally, a special note of thanks to Jim and Sheri Williams for providing a home away from home during my sometimes-lengthy visits to the state.

— J.S.

Rushing waters of the Little Miami River, Clifton Gorge State Nature Preserve, Greene County